Scottish Cookbo

Delicious Recipes from Scotland

BY

Stephanie Sharp

License Notes

Table of Contents

Introduction

People from outside Scotland often want to know the technique of preparing Scottish recipes at their homes.

If you are planning to celebrate a Scottish festival, then we can help you out with the recipes.

These recipes would tingle your taste buds and would delight your mood as well. Scotland's seafood recipes add gorgeous color to your plates and are considered to be one of the best recipes.

With this book, you can get plenty of food choices about different types of Scottish recipes that you can easily prepare for your loved ones every special occasion such as, Scottish Porridge, Scottish Breakfast Milk Punch, Kippers and Oatcakes, Potato Scones, Scottish Tattie Scones, Scottish salmon caesar salad, Tealoaf, Scottish Rabbit Curry, Scottish Shortbread, Scottish Stovies, Scottish Stuffed Mushrooms, Instant Pot Skirlie, Leek Chicken Soup, Scottish Savoury Puffs, Scottish Honey Cakes, Traditional Scottish Black Bun, Scottish Macaroon Bars, Honey and whisky mousse, and so on.

Become a master of traditional Scottish-style cooking. Just turn the pages over, and amaze your family with your cooking skills.

Breakfast

Scottish Porridge

Prep Time: 10 minutes

Cooking Time: 10 minutes

Servings: 2 persons

This recipe is very easy to prepare, very nutritious, high in dietary fiber and tastes great too!

Ingredients

- 1 tablespoon jam
- 3 tablespoons maple syrup
- 1 cup rolled oats
- 2 tablespoons brown sugar
- 1 cup milk
- Salt, as required
- 1 tablespoon fresh cream

Directions

Over moderate heat in a large pan, heat up the milk a bit and then, add in the oats & salt. Bring it to a boil and continue to cook until the porridge is thick, for a couple of minutes, stirring frequently.

Once done, decrease the heat & continue to cook for 5 to 7 minutes more.

Remove the pan from heat, set aside for a minute. Serve warm with maple syrup, brown sugar, jam and fresh cream.

Nutritional Value: kcal: 379, Fat: 7.2 g, Fiber: 4.1 g, Protein: 9.4 g

Scottish Bacon and Potato Pie

Prep Time: 20 minutes

Cooking Time: 50 minutes

Servings: 6 persons

Absolutely delicious, healthy, and quite easy to prepare! Feel free to serve this recipe with your favorite sauce on the side and enjoy.

Ingredients

- 2 pounds Idaho potatoes
- 9 slices of bacon
- 3 tablespoons butter, melted
- ¼ cup parmesan cheese
- Black pepper, freshly cracked, to taste

Directions

Coat a deep, large pie pan with the nonstick spray and then, preheat your oven to 425 F in advance.

Place the bacon strips into the bottom of your pie pan, preferably across the length & continue to add them until the sides and bottom of your dish is completely covered with meat, slightly turning the strips.

Scrub the potatoes & slice into ¼" thin pieces. Layer the potatoes on top. Sprinkle with 1/3 of parmesan cheese and then, drizzle with approximately 1 tablespoon of butter then sprinkle with cracked black pepper to taste.

Create one more layer of potatoes over the cheese layer. Repeat this cooking step for a total of three times, ending with the parmesan cheese, butter & cracked black pepper, firmly pressing the potatoes before you add the cheese layer.

Cook in the preheated oven until the potatoes are just tender, for 45 to 50 minutes in total.

Remove from the oven & let sit for a couple of minutes before transfer it onto a large serving platter. Slice into desired pieces, preferably like a pie. Serve immediately and enjoy.

Nutritional Value: kcal: 340, Fat: 22 g, Fiber: 3.1 g, Protein: 9.1 g

Scottish-Style Oatmeal with Butter

Prep Time: 10 minutes

Cooking Time: 30 minutes

Servings: 4 persons

High in dietary fiber, this recipe is very healthy and tastes delicious as well. Feel free to use a splash of cream in this recipe.

Ingredients

- 1 cup steel-cut oats
- 3 cups cold water, plus additional, if required
- Sea or kosher salt, to taste

Optional Ingredients:

- A pat of unsalted butter
- Flaky sea salt

Directions

Over high heat in a cooking pot, dry-toast the oats until roasted lightly & fragrant, stirring & tossing every now and then.

Next, combine the oats with water in the saucepan then, add the water.

Bring it to a simmer then, lightly seasoning with a pinch of salt. Once done, decrease the heat & maintain a gentle simmer, continue to cook for 5 more minutes, until the porridge is thickened well, uncovered, slowly stirring the ingredients every now and then.

Scoop the cooked porridge into bowls & top with the butter. Feel free to sprinkle your dish with the flaky salt. Serve immediately and enjoy.

Nutritional Value: kcal: 142, Fat: 2.1 g, Fiber: 3 g, Protein: 5.2 g

Scottish Breakfast Milk Punch

Prep Time: 2 minutes

Cooking Time: 2 minutes

Servings: 1 person

Just before you serve this recipe, feel free to garnish your drink with grated cinnamon.

Ingredients

- 15mL maple syrup
- 30mL cream
- 15mL apple brandy
- 45mL scotch

Directions

Shake all of the ingredients together in a cocktail shaker

Once done, strain the mix into an old-fashioned glass, preferably over fresh ice

Serve immediately and enjoy.

Nutritional Value: kcal: 220, Fat: 9 g, Fiber: 0.0 g, Protein: 0.8 g

Kippers and Oatcakes

Prep Time: 10 minutes

Cooking Time: 20 minutes

Servings: 8 persons

When I was a kid, I was in love with these kippers & oatcakes. Feel free to drizzle these delicious oatcakes with a nice squeeze of lemon.

Ingredients

- 250 g oatmeal, preferably pinhead
- ½ teaspoon baking powder
- 40 g unsalted butter
- 6 to 7 tablespoons water
- ½ teaspoon salt

Directions

Over moderate heat in a large saucepan, heat up the butter in water until melted

Combine the oats with baking powder & salt, make a well in the center in a large-sized mixing bowl until mixed well.

Immediately add the butter-water mix, continue to mix the ingredients using fingers until you get dough like consistency.

Lightly coat a large-sized baking tray with butter and preheat your oven to 400 F in advance.

Add the prepared dough into the middle of the baking tray, press out using your fingers until you get round (approximately ¼ cm thick). Score into triangles, just like shortbread.

Bake in the preheated oven until the edges begin to turn golden brown, for 20 minutes.

Serve immediately with bread or toast and enjoy

Nutritional Value: kcal: 56, Fat: 4.4 g, Fiber: 0.4 g, Protein: 0.7 g

Potato Scones

Prep Time: 20 minutes

Cooking Time: 20 minutes

Servings: 6 persons

To make these scones more flavorful, feel free to add onion powder, garlic (powdered garlic works too), and a bit of shredded cheese as well.

Ingredients

- 4 ounces self-rising flour
- 1 pound potatoes, cooked
- 2 ounces softened butter, at room temperature
- Salt, as required, to taste

Directions

Lightly coat a cast iron skillet or griddle and then, heat it over medium-high heat until hot.

Meanwhile, mash the potatoes with butter, flour & salt in a large-sized mixing bowl until you get stiff dough like consistency.

Turn the dough out onto a large work surface, preferably lightly floured. Lightly knead the dough & roll to approximately ½" thick. Make six triangular wedges from the prepared dough.

Working in batches & cook the formed scones for 3 to 4 minutes on each side, until turn golden brown, turning once.

Nutritional Value: kcal: 182, Fat: 6 g, Fiber: 2 g, Protein: 3.2 g

Scottish Breakfast Sandwich

Prep Time: 10 minutes

Cooking Time: 20 minutes

Servings: 12 persons

Feel free to sub the green onion with scallion. A perfect morning meal which would keep you full and satisfied till your next one!

Ingredients

- 2 cups all-purpose flour
- ½ cup Scottish cheddar, shredded
- 4 teaspoons baking powder
- 1/3 cup cold butter, diced
- 1 tablespoon pure honey
- ¼ cup green onions, chopped
- 1 organic egg, large-sized, for egg wash
- ¾ cup milk
- Freshly ground black pepper, to taste
- ¾ teaspoon salt

To Serve:

- Ham, arugula or spinach, fried eggs, and whole-grain mustard

Directions

Line a large-sized baking sheet with the parchment and then, preheat your oven to 450 F in advance.

Next, combine the flour with sugar, baking powder & salt in the bowl of a food processor or a large-sized mixing bowl until mixed well. Cut in the butter and continue to mix the ingredients using a fork, pastry blender, or a food processor until the mixture is crumbly. Once done, stir in the green onions, milk, and shredded cheese until the mix is just moistened.

Drop the prepared dough onto an ungreased or parchment lined baking sheet, approximately 2" apart. Brush it lightly with the beaten egg and then, sprinkle with the freshly ground black pepper, bake in the preheated oven until turn golden brown, for 12 to 15 minutes.

Slice the cooked biscuits lengthwise into half and then, serve with the serving ingredients.

Nutritional Value: kcal: 149, Fat: 6.4 g, Fiber: 0.6 g, Protein: 4.2 g

Delicious Scottish Breakfast

Prep Time: 10 minutes

Cooking Time: 50 minutes

Servings: 4 persons

Feel free to sub the butter with any of your favorite oil and serve it with baked beans, black pudding, and toast.

Ingredients

- 8 mushroom caps
- 4 pre-cooked sausages
- 2 tomatoes, large-sized, cut into eight slices
- 8 bacon slices, thin-cut
- 4 organic eggs, large-sized
- 2 tablespoons butter

Directions

Prepare the bacon per your likings. Preheat your oven to 400 F with the rack in middle position.

For easy clean up, line a large-sized rimmed baking sheet with aluminum foil.

Bake the bacon slices in the preheated oven for 5 to 7 minutes, in the pan. Once done, rotate the sheet & continue to cook until brown & crisped, for 5 to 7 more minutes.

To soak up any additional grease, immediately transfer the cooked bacon to a paper towels lined plate using a pair of tongs or fork.

Next, add mushrooms to the pan and then, toss with the bacon dripping & immediately season with the salt. Cook for 10 to 25 minutes, until the mushrooms begin to turn brown and release their liquid.

Add sausages to the hot pan and then, turn off your oven.

Meanwhile, fry the eggs to your desired likings.

Once done, plate 2 tomatoes slices along with 2 bacon slices, an egg, two roasted mushroom caps, and a sausage per plate. Season with pepper and salt, serve immediately and enjoy.

Nutritional Value: kcal: 511, Fat: 42 g, Fiber: 1 g, Protein: 22 g

Scottish Tattie Scones

Prep Time: 20 minutes

Cooking Time: 20 minutes

Servings: 8 persons

For the gluten-free version, feel free to use gluten-free flour with baking soda and for the vegan version, use vegan butter or olive oil and skip the egg.

Ingredients

- 1 egg, medium-sized
- 4 ½ ounces flour, plus more for rolling
- 1 pound baking potatoes, peeled, cooked & mashed
- 2 tablespoons melted butter, plus more for greasing
- 1 teaspoon baking powder
- ½ teaspoon salt

Directions

Preheat your oven to 400 F in advance.

Combine all of the ingredients together in a large-sized mixing bowl until you get sticky dough like consistency.

Roll the formed dough out on a floured surface to about ½" thickness.

Cut into rounds, preferably saucer-sized and then, score a cross into the dough to make four equal wedges.

Coat a large-sized baking sheet with the butter & bake the scones until risen and turn golden brown, for 20 minutes.

Serve with a pat of butter, serve immediately and enjoy.

Nutritional Value: kcal: 134, Fat: 22 g, Fiber: 4 g, Protein: 4 g

Scottish Oatcakes

Prep Time: 10 minutes

Cooking Time: 40 minutes

Servings: 8 persons

These oatcakes taste more like oat cookies. You can substitute whole wheat flour for white & use butter than shortening. Absolutely delicious and mouthwatering!

Ingredients

- ½ teaspoon baking soda
- 1 ½ cups oats, preferably old-fashioned
- ¼ cup buttermilk
- 1 cup all purpose flour
- ½ cup vegetable shortening, chilled & cut into pieces
- ¼ teaspoon salt
- ½ cup sugar

Directions

Preheat your oven to 350 F in advance. Coat two, large heavy baking sheets with butter. Add oats into a large-sized mixing bowl and then, sift the flour with baking soda, sugar and salt into the same bowl. Rub the shortening using fingertips until you get coarse meal like mixture. Add in the buttermilk, give the ingredients a good stir until you get dough like consistency. Transfer the formed dough to a well floured surface and then, roll it out into ¼" thickness.

Make rounds from the prepared batter using 2 ½" round cookie cutter. Place them on the prepared sheets, evenly spaced. Gather the scraps, reroll & cut out more of rounds.

Bake the oatcakes for 10 to 12 minutes, until edges turn pale golden. Transfer the baking sheets to wire racks & let cool for a couple of minutes. Transfer the cakes to racks to completely cool and then, store them at room temperature in an airtight container.

Nutritional Value: kcal: 269, Fat: 9 g, Fiber: 1.6 g, Protein: 6.3 g

Lunch

Scottish Raisin Scones

Prep Time: 20 minutes

Cooking Time: 20 minutes

Servings: 4 persons

I have prepared these delicious raisin scones a lot of times and each time, it was a hit. Feel free to serve it with a glass full of your favorite milk and enjoy.

Ingredients

- 1 tablespoon white vinegar
- 2 cups all-purpose flour
- 1 cup milk
- ½ teaspoon baking soda
- 3 tablespoons sugar
- 1/3 cup butter or shortening
- 1 beaten egg yolk
- ½ cup raisins
- Sugar, as required
- 1 teaspoon salt

Directions

Preheat your oven to 450 F in advance. In a medium-sized mixing bowl, stir vinegar into the milk, set the mixture aside.

Next, combine flour with baking soda, sugar and salt in a medium-sized mixing bowl, give it a good stir until blended well. Cut in the butter or shortening until you get coarse crumbs like mixture and then, stir in the raisins. Once done, immediately add the prepared milk mixture into the dry ingredients, give it a good stir using a fork until moistened, for a minute or two.

Turn it out on a large board, preferably lightly floured, gently knead for 20 times and then, place the dough on a large-sized cookie sheet, preferably ungreased. Roll or pat out to a ½"thick circle and then, cut into 8 wedges, ensure you don't separate it. Brush with the beaten egg yolk then, sprinkle with the sugar.

Bake until turn golden, for 12 to 15 minutes. Serve warm and enjoy.

Nutritional Value: kcal: 244, Fat: 9 g, Fiber: 1.2 g, Protein: 4 g

Scottish-Style Flapjacks

Prep Time: 20 minutes

Cooking Time: 40 minutes

Servings: 8 persons

This recipe tastes similar to American pancake style flapjacks. Absolutely delicious & healthy!

Ingredients

- 225 grams rolled oats
- 1/3 cup sugar
- 4 tablespoons golden syrup
- 125 grams butter
- ¼ tsp salt

Directions

Over moderate heat in a large pan, heat up the butter until melted and then, mix it with the golden syrup and then, add in the leftover ingredients.

Mix the ingredients well, pressing lightly into a 20 cm shallow tin, lightly coated with oil.

Preheat your oven to 350 F & bake for 35 to 40 minutes. Decrease the temperature and bake for a couple of more minutes.

Remove & stand let for a couple of minutes, at room temperature and then, cut carefully into desired shapes of bars.

Serve warm and enjoy.

Nutritional Value: kcal: 267, Fat: 14 g, Fiber: 2.6 g, Protein: 3.6 g

Scottish Salmon Caesar Salad

Prep Time: 10 minutes

Cooking Time: 10 minutes

Servings: 2 persons

Rather than using the salmon, you can even use shredded chicken in this recipe. Feel free to squeeze a bit of lemon juice on top.

Ingredients

- 3 lettuces, thickly sliced
- 220g pack Scottish salmon fillets
- 4 tablespoons Caesar salad dressing
- 20g garlic & herb croutons
- 2 anchovies, finely chopped
- 50g British peas, shelled
- 1 tablespoon olive oil
- Freshly ground black pepper

Directions

Over high heat in a large, nonstick frying pan, heat up the oil until hot.

Season the fish with black pepper then, carefully add it to the hot pan and fry for 2 to 3 minutes per side.

Add lettuce with 3 tablespoons of Caesar dressing, anchovies, peas and croutons to a large bowl

Combine the ingredients then, arrange in a large-sized serving dish

Once the fish is cooked, remove the skin & flake on top of the dish

Just before serving, drizzle with the leftover Caesar dressing, serve immediately and enjoy.

Nutritional Value: kcal: 481, Fat: 33 g, Fiber: 3.1 g, Protein: 26 g

Tealoaf

Prep Time: 30 minutes

Cooking Time: 20 minutes

Servings: 8 persons

Filled with dry fruits, eggs and brown sugar, this tealoaf tastes amazing. You can even serve it with a wedge of creamy blue cheese. Enjoy.

Ingredients

- 100 g soft brown sugar
- 1 heaping teaspoon of baking powder
- 225 g plain flour
- 4 eggs, free range
- 25 g muscovado sugar
- 1 teaspoon cinnamon, leveled
- 400 g dried fruit, mixed
- 125 g butter
- A pot of tea, aromatic and strong

For garnish:

- Flaked almonds

Directions

Pour the pot of tea on dried fruit in a large bowl. Set aside for overnight.

The next day, line a large-sized baking tray and then, preheat your oven to 350 F in advance.

Beat the butter with sugar then slowly add in the leftover ingredients (except fruit).

Once the mix is glossy, immediately fold in the drained fruit. Feel free to add a bit of tea, if required.

Spoon into the lined cake tin then, scatter with the almonds. Bake in the preheated oven until a metal skewer comes out clean, for 30 minutes.

Nutritional Value: kcal: 424, Fat: 14 g, Fiber: 4.6 g, Protein: 7.2 g

Delicious Baked Salmon

Prep Time: 20 minutes

Cooking Time: 20 minutes

Servings: 4 persons

Feel free to use hot smoked salmon or salmon fillets in this recipe and serve with vegetables such as broccoli.

Ingredients

- 375g smoked salmon, chopped into bite size pieces
- 2 potatoes, large-sized, peeled & chopped into small dice
- 50g peas, fresh or frozen
- 4 finely sliced spring onions
- 30 g breadcrumbs
- 200 g crème fraiche, low fat
- 1 to 2 tablespoons dill or parsley, chopped
- 30 g Scottish cheddar, grated
- 2 tablespoons milk
- Freshly ground black pepper & salt to taste

Directions

Preheat your oven to 380 F in advance. Parboil the potato pieces in salted water until soft, ensure you don't cook them. Drain well & set aside to cool it down.

Next, gently combine the salmon with peas, spring onions, soft potatoes, dill or parsley, milk and crème fraiche in a large-sized mixing bowl until mixed well.

Season with pepper and salt then, transfer the contents into an oven proof dish, preferably medium sized. Combine the cheese with breadcrumbs then, sprinkle over the prepared fish mixture, ensure it covers it nicely.

Bake until piping hot & the topping turns golden brown, for 20 minutes. Serve warm and enjoy.

Nutritional Value: kcal: 521, Fat: 27 g, Fiber: 4.1 g, Protein: 24 g

Scottish Rabbit Curry

Prep Time: 10 minutes

Cooking Time: 2 hours & 10 minutes

Servings: 4 persons

This recipe goes well with steam cooked basmati rice, I generally top the rice with the curry but you can serve it with anything you want. Absolutely delicious and mouthwatering!

Ingredients

- ½ cup Canadian or British bacon, chopped
- 1 whole rabbit, cut into small-sized pieces (2 to 2 ½ pounds)
- 2 tablespoons mild curry paste
- 1 tablespoon all-purpose flour
- 3 cups chicken broth, low-sodium
- 1 cup fresh celery, chopped
- 2 cups button mushrooms
- 1 ½ cups pearl onions
- 2 tablespoons softened butter, unsalted, at room temperature
- 1 teaspoon salt

For Serving, Optional:

- Steam cooked basmati rice

Directions

Over moderate heat in a Dutch oven, heat up the butter until melted and then, sauté the pieces of rabbit for 12 to 15 minutes, until browned well. Once done, remove from the hot pan & set aside.

Next, sauté the bacon in the same pan for 8 to 10 minutes, until browned & rendered its fat, over medium heat. Add flour & continue to cook for 2 to 3 minutes, until dissolved, whisking the ingredients every now and then. Add in the curry paste, give it a good stir until combine well. Once done, slowly stir in the chicken broth and continue to stir and cook the ingredients, over moderate heat.

Decrease the heat to medium-low & add in the set aside pieces of rabbit along with the celery, mushrooms, onions & salt. Let simmer roughly for 1 ½ hours, until the meat is cooked through, the sauce has thickened up & the onions are tender, stirring occasionally. Serve warm and enjoy.

Nutritional Value: kcal: 324, Fat: 16 g, Fiber: 2.4 g, Protein: 16 g

Scottish Smoked Salmon

Prep Time: 10 minutes

Cooking Time: 20 minutes

Servings: 2 persons

My entire family is just crazy about this delicious salmon recipe. I often serve these on the breakfast table as well and my family just loves it. Feel free to garnish your recipe with fresh rosemary.

Ingredients

- 4 slices of Scottish Smoked Salmon
- ½ cup softened cream cheese, at room temperature
- 1 tablespoon dill, fresh & minced, plus additional for garnish
- 4 soft-boiled eggs, organic, large-sized
- Zest of 1 lemon, fresh
- 4 slices of lightly toasted sourdough bread
- 1 seedless cucumber, small-sized, sliced thinly
- Freshly ground black pepper and kosher salt, as required

Directions

Combine the softened cream cheese with lemon zest, dill, and a generous pinch each of pepper and salt in a small-sized mixing bowl. Give the ingredients a good stir until spreadable & combined well.

Evenly divide the prepared cream cheese mixture among each slice of bread then, top with the cucumber slice. Once done, top each slice with a soft-boiled egg and a Scottish Salmon slice. Garnish with additional fresh dill, serve immediately and enjoy

Nutritional Value: kcal: 833, Fat: 36 g, Fiber: 4.8 g, Protein: 57 g

Scottish Shortbread

Prep Time: 20 minutes

Cooking Time: 40 minutes

Servings: 24 persons

This Scottish shortbread is just delicious! I often serve it with black tea with some butter on the side.

Ingredients

- 125g caster sugar
- 350g plain flour
- 250g softened butter, at room temperature
- A pinch of salt
- Caster sugar, for dusting

Directions

Preheat your oven to 320 F in advance. Combine the flour with sugar & salt in a large-sized mixing bowl until mixed well then, cut in the butter & add them to the bowl as well. Continue to mix the ingredients for a minute or two, until you get a dough ball (ensure you don't beat the mixture).

Evenly divide the prepared mixture into two parts & put a portion into each tin, lightly pressing into an even layer.

Once done, prick the surface using a fork.

Bake in the preheated oven until the mixture turns pale golden color, for 30 to 40 minutes, in middle.

Remove the shortbread carefully from the tins then, cut into petticoat tails, immediately transfer them to a wire rack to completely cool and then, dust with the caster sugar. Serve immediately and enjoy.

Nutritional Value: kcal: 139, Fat: 8.6 g, Fiber: 1 g, Protein: 1.2 g

Scottish Ukrainian Cabbage Rolls

Prep Time: 30 minutes

Cooking Time: 2 hours & 20 minutes

Servings: 24 persons

These cabbage rolls are one of my favorites and taste delicious too. You can even cook these rolls in Crockpot on low-heat for approximately six hours.

Ingredients

- 1 cup sliced mushrooms
- 1 pound ground beef
- 4 cups of brown rice
- 1 medium onion diced
- 2 cans gluten-free condensed tomato soup (10 oz each)
- 1 large cabbage
- 1 cup ketchup plus more to taste

Directions

Coat a large-sized roasting pan or casserole dish with non-stick cooking spray and then, preheat your oven to 250 F in advance.

Cook the cabbage for 10 minutes in microwave and then let cool. Turn & cook in the microwave for 10 more minutes.

Remove the core from cabbage & remove the cabbage leaves carefully as well. Microwave again for 5 more minutes.

Brown the chopped onion with ground beef over moderate heat in a large pan. During the last minute of cooking, add in the mushrooms & cook until onions & mushrooms turn soft and meat is well browned.

Cook the rice until cooked through.

Combine the ground beef mixture with ketchup and rice in a large-sized mixing bowl.

Roll a tablespoon of the prepared filling into the cabbage roll.

Gently place in the prepared pan & pour the tomato soup on top of the cabbage rolls. Bake until the cabbage is tender, roughly for 2 hours. Serve warm and enjoy.

Nutritional Value: kcal: 176, Fat: 3 g, Fiber: 2 g, Protein: 5.10 g

Scottish Stovies

Prep Time: 10 minutes

Cooking Time: 1 hour & 30 minutes

Servings: 8 persons

You would fall in love with this delicious stew. Just serve it with crusty bread or oatcakes and enjoy the taste.

Ingredients

- 1 ¾ pounds potatoes, peeled & cut in to 3cm cubes
- 30g butter or lard
- 2 carrots, large-sized, peeled & cut into 2cm cubes
- 1 onion, large-sized, finely chopped
- 1 ¼ pounds leftover roast meat (beef or lamb)
- ½ swede, peeled & cut into cubes (preferably 2 cm, 1 pound)
- 500ml lamb or beef stock
- 1 celery stick, finely chopped

Directions

Over moderate heat in a medium sized saucepan, heat up the butter or lard. Decrease the heat to medium-low and then, add onion, fry until softened, for 10 minutes. Add the carrot, swede & celery, continue to fry the ingredients for 5 more minutes.

Stir in the leftover meat and then, add the potatoes. Slowly pour the stock on top and generously season to taste, bring the mixture to a boil. Once done, decrease the heat further to a simmer. Cover & cook until the potatoes have broken down completely and vegetables have softened, for 1 hour and 30 minutes. Serve warm and enjoy.

Nutritional Value: kcal: 449, Fat: 28 g, Fiber: 2 g, Protein: 24 g

Dinner

Scottish Stuffed Mushrooms

Prep Time: 10 minutes

Cooking Time: 20 minutes

Servings: 4 persons

Absolutely delicious and healthy! Feel free to garnish the mushroom caps with finely chopped cilantro and enjoy. You can even squeeze a bit of lemon on top as well.

Ingredients

- 4 flat Portobello mushrooms, large-sized, clean
- 1 cooked vegetarian haggis
- 75g grated veggie cheddar
- A bit of vegetable oil, for brushing
- Optional Ingredients:
- 20g pine nuts

Directions

Preheat your grill over medium heat in advance. Coat the mushrooms lightly with oil using a brush & fry over moderate heat in a large frying pan, for a minute or two per side, until just cooked.

Place the mushrooms on the preheated grill pan, gills up and then, fill with the vegetarian haggis (mixed with the optional pine nuts). Once done, immediately top with the grated cheese.

Cook under the grill until the cheese has started to turn brown & bubbling. Serve immediately and enjoy.

Nutritional Value: kcal: 228, Fat: 19 g, Fiber: 1.2 g, Protein: 11 g

Scottish Curry

Prep Time: 20 minutes

Cooking Time: 55 minutes

Servings: 6 persons

You will fall in love with this delicious recipe just like I have fallen in love with it. Feel free to serve it with rice, veggies, flat breads, chutneys, and so on.

Ingredients

- 5 pounds chicken legs (roughly 10 to 12 pieces)
- 1 large onion, peeled & thinly sliced
- 2 tablespoons all-purpose flour
- 1 tablespoon turmeric, freshly grated
- 12 ounces thick-cut bacon, cut into ¼" strips
- 1 head of garlic cloves, roasted, squeezed from the skins
- 2 heaping tablespoons curry powder, store-bought or homemade
- 1 to 2 tablespoons Porcini mushrooms, finely ground
- 2 tablespoons white wine vinegar
- 1 cup pearl onions, peeled
- 3 cups chicken stock
- 1 teaspoon black pepper, freshly ground
- A large pinch of ground cayenne pepper

Directions

Over moderate heat in a wide, large, heavy skillet, cook the bacon. Remove the cooked bacon to a plate lined with paper towel, leaving the fat inside the hot pan.

Raise the heat, work in batches and brown the chicken legs. Once done, remove them to a large-sized rimmed dish.

Decrease the heat to medium low and then, immediately add in the garlic, sliced onions, turmeric, cayenne, and pepper, sauté until the onions have softened, for a minute or two.

Stir in the flour followed by ground Porcinis, and curry powder. Once done, add the pearl onions, chicken stock and the kept-aside bacon and chicken.

Bring the curry to a boil, cover and decrease the heat to a simmer. Continue to cook until the chicken is done, for 30 more minutes. Remove from the heat & stir in the white wine vinegar.

Serve immediately and enjoy.

Nutritional Value: kcal: 561, Fat: 26 g, Fiber: 1.2 g, Protein: 6.1 g

Scottish Chicken Tikka Masala

Prep Time: 20 minutes

Cooking Time: 1 hour & 30 minutes

Servings: 4 persons

I generally serve this tikka masala with basmati rice, sprinkled with fresh coriander but you can serve it per your likings.

Ingredients

- 1 teaspoon ground coriander
- 2 pounds boneless chicken thighs, cut into half
- 1 teaspoon kashmiri chili powder
- 5 tablespoons yoghurt, full-fat
- 1 teaspoon ground cumin
- ½ teaspoon tandoori masala
- 1 tablespoon garlic & ginger paste
- ½ teaspoon garam masala
- 1 teaspoon Turmeric
- ½ teaspoon chili powder
- 1 teaspoon madras curry powder
- Juice of ½ lemon, fresh
- 1 pound potatoes, cut into small chunks & par boiled for a couple of minutes in salted water
- 1 teaspoon black cumin seeds
- 2 black cardamom
- 1 tablespoon kasoori methi
- ¾ pounds finely chopped onion
- 1 teaspoon ginger and garlic paste
- 2 bay leaves
- 1 inch cinnamon stick
- ½ teaspoon garam masala
- 100 ml water
- Fresh coriander
- 1 tin cream of tomato soup

- 3 tablespoons coconut oil
- Salt, as required, to taste

Directions

Combine the yoghurt with tandoori masala, garlic paste, ginger, kashmiri chill powder, ground coriander, cumin, turmeric, chill powder, garam masala, oil, lemon juice, and salt in a large mixing bowl until mixed well. Place the potatoes and chicken in the bowl, continue to mix the ingredients until nicely coated, set aside and let marinate for a couple of hours.

Place the marinated potatoes and chicken on a large-sized baking tray, lightly an oiled & bake until cooked through, for 45 to 50 minutes.

Next, over moderate heat in a large wok, heat up the coconut oil until hot. Once done, add the black cardamoms, cumin seeds, bay leaves & cinnamon stick. Once sizzling, immediately add in the chopped onions & continue to fry the ingredients until turn golden brown, for 15 minutes, stirring the ingredients every now and then.

Add a teaspoon of garlic and ginger paste & continue to fry for 2 more minutes, stirring frequently.

Add the tomato sauce, tablespoon of Kasoori Methi, and salt to taste, let simmer for a couple of minutes.

Add the juices from baking tray & leftover marinade from the bowl (add 100ml of water to the bowl and pour the content), let simmer for a couple of minutes.

Add the potato and chicken pieces, cover & let simmer for a couple of more minutes. Add some fresh coriander and ½ teaspoon of garam masala, give the ingredients a good stir and continue to cook for half a minute more.

Just before serving, don't forget to remove the bay leaves, black cardamom & cinnamon stick. Enjoy.

Nutritional Value: kcal: 574, Fat: 26 g, Fiber: 6.6g, Protein: 46 g

Scottish Lamb Stew

Prep Time: 20 minutes

Cooking Time: 2 hours & 10 minutes

Servings: 6 persons

Absolutely delish! Feel free to add ½ cup of cooked barley to the stew & serve on the mashed tatties.

Ingredients

For Stew:

- 2 cloves of garlic, crushed
- ½ pound diced turnip
- 2 large carrots, diced
- 1 white onion diced
- 2 ½ pounds lamb leg or lamb collarbutt, cut into 1" cubes
- 2 sprigs of parsley
- 8 mushrooms, cut into half
- 2 tablespoons tomato paste
- 1 bay leaf
- 2 tablespoons flour
- 350 ml each of orange juice, and vegetable stock
- 2 tablespoons olive oil
- Pepper and salt to taste

For Dumplings

- 25 cups self raising flour
- 2 tablespoons parsley chopped
- ½ cup milk
- 60 g cold butter cubed

Directions

Season the meat and then, sear over medium to high heat in Dutch oven for 5 minutes.

Remove the meat & place it on a large, clean plate.

Cook the vegetables (but don't add the mushrooms) for 2 to 3 minutes, over medium heat

Add the meat along with any juices into the pot again.

Add flour followed by the tomato paste, give the ingredients a good stir & continue to cook for 2 to 3 more minutes.

Add in the stock, orange juice, thyme & bayleaf to the pot. Cover & cook until lamb is just tender, for 1 ½ hours, on low-heat.

Add the button mushrooms then, spoon the dumpling batter on it. Cover & cook on low heat until dumplings are cooked through, for 20 more minutes.

For Dumplings

In a large-sized mixing bowl, add flour then, rub in the butter using your fingers until you get fine bread crumbs like mixture.

Make a well in middle then, pour in the milk followed by the parsley, gently stir the ingredients & spoon into the cooked stew.

Nutritional Value: kcal: 441, Fat: 36 g, Fiber: 2 g, Protein: 38 g

Instant Pot Skirlie

Prep Time: 10 minutes

Cooking Time: 10 minutes

Servings: 8 persons

Rather than using the turkey broth and drippings, feel free to use chicken broth & drippings. Absolutely delicious and mouthwatering!

Ingredients

- 2 cup pin head oats or steel cut oats
- ½ cup turkey drippings
- 75 cups turkey broth
- 2 tablespoons softened butter, at room temperature
- 4 teaspoons fresh thyme, chopped
- 1/8 teaspoon sea salt
- 2 brown or yellow onion, large-sized, roughly chopped

Directions

Preheat an instant pot by selecting the Sauté feature.

Once hot, add in the butter, onions and turkey drippings, sauté the ingredients roughly for 4 minutes.

Add oats & continue to sauté the ingredients until most of liquid is absorbed.

Add the broth followed by thyme & salt, deglaze the pot well.

Close the lid & cook for 4 minutes at high pressure. Once the cooking cycle completes, wait about 10 minutes, then let the pressure to release naturally.

Carefully remove the lid & let simmer until the skirlie turns dry.

Nutritional Value: kcal: 216, Fat: 6.2 g, Fiber: 4 g, Protein: 8.1 g

Scottish Oat & Leek Pilaf with Salmon

Prep Time: 20 minutes

Cooking Time: 45 minutes

Servings: 4 persons

This recipe is very nutritious and healthy. The additional lemon juice that you squeeze on top of it, gives the recipe a nice and tangy taste!

Ingredients

- 4 piece salmon fillet, skinless (approximately ½"thick)
- 1 cup steel-cut oats rinsed
- 2 leeks, chopped (only light green and white part)
- ½ lemon
- 2 cups milk
- ¾ cup vegetable or chicken broth, low-sodium
- 1 teaspoon dried dill or 2 tablespoons fresh dill, chopped
- 2 cups green beans or asparagus, chopped
- 1 tablespoon butter
- Pepper
- ½ teaspoon salt
- More of fresh dill, chopped, optional

Directions

Over medium heat in a large, deep skillet, heat up the butter until melted and then, sauté the chopped leeks with ¼ teaspoon pepper & salt for a minute or two. Decrease the heat, cover & cook until leeks have started to turn golden and are soft, for 8 minutes, stirring the ingredients every now and then. Once done, immediately stir in the oats.

Stir in the milk and broth, increase the heat a bit and bring it to a simmer, stirring the ingredients every now and then. Once done, decrease the heat again to low, cover & let simmer until oats are tender slightly, for 10 to 12 minutes, stirring once.

In the meantime, finely grate the lemon zest and cut the lemon into four wedges.

Stir the lemon zest with dill and asparagus into the oats. Nestle the salmon fillets into the oats, evenly spaced and then, season with pepper. Cover & let simmer until salmon is just opaque and releases white juices, for 10 minutes. Immediately remove it from the heat & let stand for 5 minutes, covered. Evenly divide the portions among the plates, serve with more of lemon wedges and sprinkled with more of dill.

Nutritional Value: kcal: 247, Fat: 8.6 g, Fiber: 1 g, Protein: 6 g

Salmon in Whisky Cream Sauce

Prep Time: 10 minutes

Cooking Time: 20 minutes

Servings: 2 persons

Feel free to garnish your dish with more of chives, serve immediately with mashed potatoes & green vegetables like peas or broccoli. Absolutely delicious and healthy!

Ingredients

- 2 plain organic salmon fillets, defrosted per the packages direction
- 1 teaspoon Dijon mustard
- 1 ½ tablespoon peppercorns, crushed
- 30ml Scotch whisky
- 15g butter
- 1 tablespoon fresh chives, finely chopped
- 120ml double cream

Directions

Coat the fillets with mustard over and then press the peppercorns into the top side of each one until nicely coated. Once done, season the fillets with a bit of salt.

Over moderate heat in a large, frying pan or heavy skillet, heat up the butter until melted. Once done, add the salmon fillets, skin-side down carefully into the hot pan with the melted butter.

Decrease the heat to medium & continue to cook the fillets for 3 to 5 minutes. Once done, transfer the fillets to a warm plate & cover lightly with aluminum foil.

It's time to prepare the sauce now. Increase the heat again & immediately but carefully add the whisky. Bring it to a boil, continue to cook until decreased by half.

Next, add the cream & give it a good stir using a large wooden spoon, combine the sauce & scrape up any bits from the bottom of your pan.

Bring the sauce to a boil again & let simmer until thickened, for a minute or two. Taste & season with more of salt and pepper as needed and then, stir in the chopped chives.

Arrange the cooked fillets carefully on warm serving plates and top with the prepared sauce. Serve and enjoy.

Nutritional Value: kcal: 267, Fat: 8.2 g, Fiber: 1.4 g, Protein: 6.2 g

Leek Chicken Soup

Prep Time: 20 minutes

Cooking Time: 1 hour & 30 minutes

Servings: 6 persons

This soup is very delicious and considered to be the Scotland's national soup and is generally served on holidays like St. Andrews Dinner, Hogmanay or Burns Supper. Feel free to garnish your soup with anything you desired. It goes well with steamed cooked basmati rice!

Ingredients

- 3 pieces of leeks, sliced
- 1 small chicken piece, cut further into small pieces
- 20 g celeriac, peeled & chopped
- 1 tea cup barley
- 100 g Prunes
- A pinch of black pepper
- 4 cups chicken broth
- 1 tablespoon salt
- 2 tablespoons butter
- A few stems of fresh parsley, chopped

Directions

Over moderate heat in a large pan, heat up the butter until melted. Once done, cook the leeks with chicken pieces, celeriac, and barley for a minute or two.

Once done, add the prunes followed by chicken broth, give it a good stir and then, sprinkle with pepper and salt to taste. Continue to cook the ingredients for a couple of more minutes, until cooked through.

Next, sprinkle with the freshly chopped parsley and cook for a minute more.

Just before serving, remove the prunes, serve warm and enjoy.

Nutritional Value: kcal: 290, Fat: 10 g, Fiber: 2 g, Protein: 3 g

Scottish Beef Stew

Prep Time: 20 minutes

Cooking Time: 4 hours & 10 minutes

Servings: 6 persons

For more heat, feel free to sprinkle black pepper and a pinch of red chili on top.

Ingredients

- 2 ½ pounds stewing beef/Aberdeen angus braising beef, chopped into bite-size chunks
- 2 tablespoons cranberry sauce or red currant jelly
- 3 garlic cloves, peeled & crushed
- 2 large onions, peeled & chopped
- 2 carrots, large-sized, peeled & chopped
- ½ small swede, peeled & chopped
- 2 teaspoons dark brown sugar
- 500 ml red wine
- 2 tablespoons tomato puree
- 1 tablespoon Worcestershire sauce
- 2 tablespoons all purpose flour mixed with a pinch of pepper and salt
- 4 bay leaves
- 2 tablespoons vegetable oil
- 700 ml beef stock - water plus 2 stock cubes is fine
- 2 potatoes, medium-sized, peeled & chopped
- ¾ teaspoon each of crushed black pepper & salt

To serve:

- Fresh thyme sprigs
- Chunks of fresh bread

Directions

Preheat your oven to 325 F in advance.

Next, over moderate heat in a large pan, heat up the oil until hot. Once done, dust the beef chunks with the flour until nicely coated & fry until all sides turn golden brown, for 7 to 8 minutes. Add the onions & continue to cook for 5 more minutes and then, stir in the garlic. Add the cranberry sauce and then, pour in the red wine, let simmer for a couple of minutes, over moderate heat.

Add in the swede, tomato puree, potatoes, carrots, stock, bay leaves, Worcestershire sauce, sugar, pepper and salt, give the ingredients a good stir. Bring mixture to a gentle boil and then, cover with a lid, continue to cook for 3 to 4 hours in the oven, stirring a few times during the cooking process.

Serve immediately with some freshly cut bread and topped with a bit of fresh thyme. Enjoy

Nutritional Value: kcal: 329, Fat: 8 g, Fiber: 4 g, Protein: 6.3 g

Scottish Savoury Puffs

Prep Time: 20 minutes

Cooking Time: 20 minutes

Servings: 6 persons

This recipe is just perfect for burns night or even bonfire night. You can even use normal milk in this recipe and can sub the wholegrain mustard with tomato puree.

Ingredients

- 1 pound vegetarian haggis
- ½ cup frozen peas
- 1 roll puff pastry
- 2 to 3 tablespoons wholegrain mustard
- ½ cup sweetcorn, frozen
- 1 tablespoon soya milk

Directions

Remove the puff pastry from your fridge and bring it to room temperature.

Next, preheat your oven to 375 F in advance.

Roll the puff pastry out on a large board, preferably lightly floured until quite thin.

Make circles from the pastry using a small cereal bowl or saucer.

Spread a bit of mustard on the pastry & then, add a filling of veggie haggis. Once done, scatter with the sweetcorn and frozen peas.

Wet the edges of formed circle lightly with a bit of water and then, fold, pressing down the edges & crimp using your fingers.

Slash the top of every puff a few times and let the steam to come out & pop onto the baking tray.

Coat each puff lightly with the milk using a brush & bake until turn golden, for 20 more minutes. Serve warm and enjoy.

Nutritional Value: kcal: 324, Fat: 19 g, Fiber: 3 g, Protein: 17 g

Desserts

Scottish Honey Cakes

Prep Time: 20 minutes

Cooking Time: 20 minutes

Servings: 14 persons

Feel free to use any of your favorite nuts in this recipe. Absolutely delicious and healthy with the anti-inflammatory health benefits of honey!

Ingredients

- 3 1/3 tablespoons sugar
- 2/5 cup flour
- 3 1/3 tablespoons margarine or butter
- 1/3 cup pure honey
- 1 organic eggs, large-sized
- 3 1/3 tablespoons walnuts
- 2 tablespoons ground hazelnuts
- ½ teaspoon baking soda
- 2 tablespoons oil
- 2/5 cup powdered sugar

Directions

Preheat your oven to 365 F in advance.

Next, over low heat in a large pan, heat up the honey with margarine and sugar, ensure you don't bring the mixture to a boil, stirring frequently.

Remove from the heat and then, add in the flour with ground walnuts, egg and baking soda.

Give the ingredients a good stir & evenly distribute the mix into 14 muffin cups, lightly coated with oil. Once done, bake in the preheated oven for 12 to 15 minutes.

Using a kitchen towel, cover & set aside at room temperature to completely cool.

Combine the powdered sugar with a bit of water until you thick glaze like consistency. Once done, smear the prepared mix on the cooled cakes and then, sprinkle with ground hazelnuts in middle. Serve immediately and enjoy.

Nutritional Value: kcal: 123, Fat: 6.7 g, Fiber: 0.2 g, Protein: 1.2 g

Chocolate Oat Cakes

Prep Time: 20 minutes

Cooking Time: 20 minutes

Servings: 20 persons

If desired, you can even add a layer of melted chocolate on top of each cooked oat cakes.

Ingredients

- ½ cup old-fashioned rolled oats
- 2/3 cup all-purpose flour
- ¼ cup hazelnuts, finely chopped
- 1/3 cup Dutch-process cocoa powder
- ½ cup softened unsalted butter, (1 stick)
- ¼ teaspoon ground cinnamon
- ½ teaspoon cardamom, freshly ground
- ¼ cup wheat germ
- ¾ cup sugar
- 2 organic egg yolks, large-sized
- 1/8 teaspoon fine salt

Directions

Line two standard-sized mini muffin tins with mini muffin liners and then, preheat your oven to 350 F in advance. Lightly coat the liners with a bit of nonstick spray then, sprinkle the bottom of each coated muffin liner with hazelnuts.

Next, whisk the cocoa with flour, oats, wheat germ, spices & salt in a medium-sized mixing bowl.

Once done, beat the butter with sugar in a separate bowl for a minute or two, until combined well, on medium speed using an electric mixer. Slowly add in the egg yolks & continue to beat the ingredients together. Add all of the dry ingredients & continue to mix the ingredients until just combined.

Scoop approximately a tablespoon of the prepared dough into the mini muffin tins over the nuts. Bake in the preheated oven for 12 to 15 minutes, until the nuts are toasty and cookies are cooked through. Transfer the cooked cookies to a wire rack to completely cool. Serve and enjoy

Nutritional Value: kcal: 227, Fat: 11 g, Fiber: 1.6 g, Protein: 3.2 g

Traditional Scottish Black Bun

Prep Time: 10 minutes

Cooking Time: 50 minutes

Servings: 20 persons

You would surely like the taste of this recipe. Feel free to sub the butter with cashew or peanut butter. It really tastes great when served warm.

Ingredients

For The Pastry

- 3 ounces lard
- ½ teaspoon baking powder
- 3 ounces margarine or butter
- A pinch of salt
- 12 ounces plain flour
- Cold water

For The Filling:

- 1 dessertspoon milk
- 2 tablespoon brandy
- 1 pound raisins, seedless
- 2 ounces blanched almonds, chopped
- 1 pound cleaned currants
- 3 ounces soft brown sugar
- 1 ½ cups plain flour
- 2 ounces mixed peel, chopped
- ½ teaspoon ground ginger
- 1 teaspoon ground allspice
- ½ teaspoon ground cinnamon
- 1 organic egg, large-sized, beaten well
- ½ teaspoon baking powder
- A generous pinch of black pepper

Directions

Coat a loaf tin, preferably 8" lightly with butter. Rub the fats into the flour & salt, mix well and then, slowly add in cold water. Continue to mix the ingredients until stiff dough like consistency is formed. Roll the pastry out & cut into six even-sized pieces, pressing it into the tin and pressing the overlaps to seal the shell of pastry.

Next, combine the raisins with almonds, currants, sugar and peel together in a large-sized mixing bowl. Sift in the flour followed by the baking powder & spices, bind them together using most of the egg and the brandy. Add milk enough to moisten.

Place the filling into the lined tin and then, add the pastry lid, pinching down the edges & seal using egg or milk. Next, using a fork, prick the surface lightly & using a skewer, make four holes to the bottom of your tin.

Create the glaze by brushing the top with leftover egg or milk.

Bake until a skewer comes out clean, for 2 to 3 hours.

Let cool in the tin & place onto a wire rack to completely cool.

Nutritional Value: kcal: 370, Fat: 11 g, Fiber: 2 g, Protein: 8 g

Scottish Butter Ice Cream

Prep Time: 10 minutes

Cooking Time: 1 hour & 30 minutes

Servings: 4 persons

You can even add a few good quality chocolate chips or any of your favorite fruit into this recipe.

Ingredients

- 285 milliliters milk, lukewarm
- 60 grams unsalted, softened butter
- 2 organic eggs, large-sized
- 6 tablespoons brown sugar
- ½ teaspoon vanilla extract
- 75 grams superfine sugar
- 300 milliliters heavy whipping cream

Directions

Over moderate heat in a large, heavy stock pot, heat up the butter until melted and then, add in the brown sugar, give it a good stir. Increase the heat & let it bubble for a minute. Once done, remove the pot from heat & let slightly cool.

Once done, pour in the lukewarm milk & place it over low heat again, continue to cook for 20 minutes, stirring the ingredients every now and then. Let completely cool.

Next, whisk the eggs with vanilla extract, and sugar in a large-sized mixing bowl. Pour this mix into the first mixture & slowly cook on low heat, ensure that you don't bring it to a boil, stirring the ingredients every now and then. Let completely cool.

Whisk the heavy whipping cream separately in a medium-sized mixing bowl until you get stiff peaks. Fold this carefully into the original mix.

Fill the ice cream maker with everything and follow the instructions provided by the manufacturer.

Pour into a container & freeze for a couple of hours.

Nutritional Value: kcal: 565, Fat: 40 g, Fiber: 0.1 g, Protein: 6 g

Scottish Macaroon Bars

Prep Time: 30 minutes

Cooking Time: 4 hours & 10 minutes

Servings: 20 persons

My family just loved the taste of these delicious bars. I often prepare it post-lunch since I have plenty of free time. However, you can try it anytime you want.

Ingredients

- 2 cups desiccated coconut
- 9 oz. chocolate, any of your favorite
- 4 cups powdered /Icing sugar
- 1 teaspoon vanilla extract
- 140 g white potatoes

Directions

Wash the potato under cold running tap water and then, bring it to a boil until you can easily cut it using a fork. Set aside and let completely cool.

Peel the potato & mash in a large-sized mixing bowl until no lumps remain.

Add approximately ¼ of sugar & continue to combine the ingredients until mixed well.

Add in the vanilla & give it a good stir.

Continue to add the powdered sugar slowly until you have utilized it completely.

Transfer the prepared mix into a baking paper lined dish, preferably freezer-proof & smooth sides. Freeze the mix for an hour or two.

Once done, remove the mix from dish & carefully remove the baking paper.

Next, using your hands, cut the mix into 20 rectangles or small bars.

Place the bars onto a baking tray lined with baking paper & freeze for an hour more.

Meanwhile, over a medium-high heat in a dry frying pan, place half of the desiccated coconut. Cook until it turns golden brown, stirring frequently. Mix the toasted coconut with the leftover desiccated coconut.

Just before you remove the bars from freezer, heat up the chocolate in a large bowl until melted.

Dip the bars carefully into the melted chocolate, ensure each bar is nicely coated & roll it immediately into the prepared coconut. Place on a wire rack until set. Once done, freeze until the chocolate is firm, for an hour or two.

Nutritional Value: kcal: 212, Fat: 8 g, Fiber: 1.6 g, Protein: 1.4 g

Scottish Toffee

Prep Time: 10 minutes

Cooking Time: 30 minutes

Servings: 20 persons

Once you are done with the toffees, you can sprinkle a bit of the optional sea salt on top.

Ingredients

- 1 ½ packages (18 ounces) semisweet chocolate chips, divided in two
- 1 cup almonds, finely chopped, divided in two
- 2 sticks (approximately 1 cup) unsalted butter
- 1 teaspoon vanilla extract
- A pinch of kosher salt
- 1 cup generously packed brown sugar

Optional Ingredients:

- Sea salt

Directions

Put half of the chocolate chips & half of the nuts onto a large-sized cookie sheet.

Next, cook brown sugar and butter in medium-sized pot over medium-high heat for 12 to 15 minutes, until you reach "hard crack" stage, stirring the ingredients every now and then.

Once done, remove the pot immediately from heat & quickly add vanilla and salt.

Pour the hot caramel mixture carefully on top of the chocolate and nuts, ensure both are nicely covered. Sprinkle with leftover chocolate. Once melted, smooth it out using the back of large-sized spoon and then, sprinkle with the leftover nuts, pressing gently into the toffee.

Nutritional Value: kcal: 413, Fat: 32 g, Fiber: 2.2 g, Protein: 3.1 g

Summer Pudding with Scottish Berries

Prep Time: 20 minutes

Cooking Time: 20 minutes

Servings: 6 persons

My family just loves the taste of this pudding. Just before serving, I top my dish with fresh berries. Absolutely delicious and delicious!

Ingredients

- 150 g blackcurrants
- 300 g strawberries, hulled & cut into quaters
- 8 slices of white bread
- 100 ml water
- 125 g sugar
- 250 g raspberries

Directions

Bring the fruit to a gentle simmer (over moderate heat in a large saucepan with enough of water). Let simmer for 2 to 3 minutes and then, add in the sugar, give it a good stir until the sugar is completely dissolved. Set the mix aside at room temperature to cool down.

Next, using a cling film or plastic wrap, line the basin of pudding.

Remove the crusts from white bread. Once done, cut a circle out using a cookie cutter & put it in place.

Place the slices of bread around the inside of your bowl, cutting small pieces to fill any gaps, leaving two slices for top.

Spoon the fruit along with a bit of juice into the bowl lined with bread.

Cover with the leftover bread, cover the bread using the overlapping cling wrap.

Cover the wrapped pudding with a saucer & place it in a larger bowl and then, put some weight over the saucer.

Place in the fridge & set aside for overnight.

Strain the leftover juice into a clean, large pan and bring it to a boil, over moderate heat. Continue to cook for a minute. Set aside for 5 minutes to cool down and then pour into the jug. Cover & put in the fridge.

To Serve

Just half an hour before you plan to serve, remove the pudding from fridge. Remove the wrap carefully and turn the prepared pudding on to a large-sized serving plate.

Pour some of the leftover juice onto a small bowl or saucer and coat the outside of bread with the juice using a pastry brush, ensure that there aren't any white patches on it.

Cut into desired slices & serve with the leftover juice & cream.

Nutritional Value: kcal: 234, Fat: 1.4 g, Fiber: 4.2 g, Protein: 4.2 g

Traditional Scottish Tablet

Prep Time: 10 minutes

Cooking Time: 30 minutes

Servings: 24 persons

Absolutely delicious! Feel free to add 1 to 2 tablespoons of Scottish whisky in this recipe.

Ingredients

- 4 ½ cups granulated sugar
- 1 cup whole milk
- 6 tablespoons unsalted butter, chopped into 1" pieces
- 1 can condensed milk, sweetened
- A pinch of salt

Directions

Coat a large-sized pan nicely with butter, set aside until required.

Next, over medium heat in a very large pan, heat up the milk with sugar until sugar is completely dissolved, stirring the ingredients occasionally.

Once done, add and stir the butter until melted.

Now, add in the sweetened condensed milk, continue to mix the ingredients until mixed well. Raise the heat & continue to stir the ingredients, bring the mixture to a boil. Continue to cook for a couple of more minutes.

Remove the pan carefully from heat & add in the optional whisky. Beat the mix carefully using a large wooden spoon for 5 to 7 more minutes.

Transfer to the firstly prepared pan, evenly spreading to the corners / edges.

Set aside for overnight to set. Enjoy.

Nutritional Value: kcal: 126, Fat: 4 g, Fiber: 0.4 g, Protein: 4 g

Chocolate Tiffin

Prep Time: 10 minutes

Cooking Time: 1 hour & 10 minutes

Servings: 12 persons

I often serve this delicious Scottish Tiffin's with a small peg of Scottish whiskey, but you can serve it with anything you want. You can store them in an airtight container for up to 2 weeks in a fridge.

Ingredients

- 2 cups semi-sweet chocolate chips
- ⅔ cup dried fruit such as raisins, candied orange & dried cranberries
- 2 tablespoons sugar
- ½ cup cubed butter
- 2 tablespoons corn syrup
- 1 ¼ cups crushed ginger snap crumbs
- 4 teaspoon cocoa powder

Directions

Over low heat in a large saucepan, heat up the butter until melted and then, add the sugar followed by cocoa, and corn syrup, continue to cook and stir the ingredients for a minute or two. Add in the dried fruit and cookie crumbs, continue to cook and mix the ingredients until thoroughly combined. Spread the prepared mix into a large pan.

Next, heat up chocolate chips in a microwave-safe bowl until chocolate is completely melted, in 30 seconds intervals, stirring after each interval.

Evenly spread the melted chocolate on top of the cookie mixture & let rest in a refrigerator for an hour.

Once done, remove from the refrigerator & let sit for a couple of minutes then, cut into desired squares. Serve and enjoy.

Nutritional Value: kcal: 191, Fat: 12 g, Fiber: 1 g, Protein: 4 g

Honey & Whisky Mousse

Prep Time: 10 minutes

Cooking Time: 3 hours & 30 minutes

Servings: 3 persons

Nothing can beat the taste of this mousse. Feel free to garnish your glass with a bit of fresh juicy raspberries & serve with shortbread!

Ingredients

- 4 gelatine leaves, soaked in cold water
- 140ml Scottish whisky
- 400ml double cream
- 1 heaping tablespoon of Scottish heather honey
- 4 organic eggs, large-sized

Directions

Place the honey with eggs & ¾ of whisky in a heatproof bowl placed over a large saucepan of barely simmering water. Carefully whisk the ingredients using an electric whisk until the mix is pale & mousse-y. Once done, set the mix aside and let cool down at room temperature.

Next, whisk the cream until stiff then, immediately whisk in the leftover whisky. Once done, fold cream into the honey-egg mixture

Squeeze any excess water from the gelatine & dissolve in a splash of hot water

Evenly divide the prepared mix between three martini glasses & let them rest in the fridge for 3 hours.

Nutritional Value: kcal: 604, Fat: 40 g, Fiber: 0 g, Protein: 10 g

Conclusion

Thank you again for choosing this book.

There is no dough in saying that Scottish recipes are the healthiest and tastiest recipes in the world today. As mentioned above, this book would help you become a master of Scottish recipes. With the detailed instructions, you can prepare these recipes quite easily.

This book would also help you in saving plenty of dollars that you may spend on Scottish recipes.

What are you still waiting for? If you haven't bought this book yet, then do it now, turn the pages, and surprise your guests with your cooking techniques.

About the Author

Born in New Germantown, Pennsylvania, Stephanie Sharp received a Masters degree from Penn State in English Literature. Driven by her passion to create culinary masterpieces, she applied and was accepted to The International Culinary School of the Art Institute where she excelled in French cuisine. She has married her cooking skills with an aptitude for business by opening her own small cooking school where she teaches students of all ages.

Stephanie's talents extend to being an author as well and she has written over 400 e-books on the art of cooking and baking that include her most popular recipes.

Sharp has been fortunate enough to raise a family near her hometown in Pennsylvania where she, her husband and children live in a beautiful rustic house on an extensive piece of land. Her other passion is taking care of the furry members of her family which include 3 cats, 2 dogs and a potbelly pig named Wilbur.

Watch for more amazing books by Stephanie Sharp coming out in the next few months.

Author's Afterthoughts

I am truly grateful to you for taking the time to read my book. I cherish all of my readers! Thanks ever so much to each of my cherished readers for investing the time to read this book!

With so many options available to you, your choice to buy my book is an honour, so my heartfelt thanks at reading it from beginning to end!

I value your feedback, so please take a moment to submit an honest and open review on Amazon so I can get valuable insight into my readers' opinions and others can benefit from your experience.

Thank you for taking the time to review!

Stephanie Sharp

For announcements about new releases, please follow my author page on Amazon.com!

You can find that at:

https://www.amazon.com/author/stephanie-sharp

*or Scan **QR-code** below.*

Printed in Great Britain
by Amazon